ENGAGE

Totally Simple Bible Studies for Teen Girls

moretobe.com

BRINGING OUT
YOUR GOD-COLOR

a bible study on life
purpose for teen girls

Elisa Pulliam
founder of moretobe.com

Dedication

For my children,
Leah, Abby, Luke, and Kaitlyn.
May you always know how
you've been intentionally chosen
by your Father in Heaven
to shine your unique
God-colors in this world.

Table of Contents

Brightly Colored

because your part matters

Did you know that your generation is often called the Mosaics? While it's not quite as popular as referring to you as the Millenials, I like it a whole lot better. Maybe that's because I have this thing for mosaics as a beautiful art form as much as I have this thing for loving spending time with teen girls.

Oh yes, it was in my college years that I finally admitted my love of art and finally declared it as a second major after realizing I had taken enough credits to satisfy that requirement. It was around the same time that I had become a Christian by putting my faith in Jesus as my Savior (more on that story later) and also discovered that I could plug into a youth group at my local church as a way to come alongside teens who struggled much like I did at their age.

I was a mess when I was teen and in desperate need of a mentor, but finding one was hard, especially without a church. However, there was this one lady who worked in the nurse's office at my high school. She would always have a warm smile and listening ear for my must-be-processed-out-loud teen drama. So, I became that girl who managed to find her way to the nurse's office daily, just because I needed that dose of love poured out on me. She left her mark on my life, setting an example for me in how I wanted to leave my mark on others—especially this generation of teen girls . . . and especially on you.

I admit, teen girls are my favorite group of people, even after 18 years spent living at a boarding school (my husband is a high school chemistry teacher, thus the whole boarding school experience) and now being in the throes of mentoring my own teen daughters. From a mom's persepctive, I really see a side of life that I never did before, and I am even more certain you need to be loved on, given space to think and explore what you believe for yourself, while also being challenged to mature in your faith and rise up as you discover opportunities to leave your mark on this world. That's why I bring you *Mosaic*.

Finding Your God Color

Have you ever seen a mosaic up close? Mosaics are made with either pieces of cut glass or broken shards of glass laid in cement to create a beautiful image. While one piece of glass may be independently beautiful, it is stunning to see how that same piece can become part of a composition to form something magnificent. And, sometimes, it's the broken pieces that lend themselves to the best use, because they fit exactly into an empty spot.

I think that is true of you and your generation, because most of you are broken pieces of glass . . . and I say that lovingly. You're broken because you live in this day and age. Your world continues to be in turmoil, and likely, your own family has endured dysfunction that masks as normal. Isn't it true that everyone knows someone who has experienced the impact of divorce? But even if it feels normal, it's not supposed to be that way!

The breakdown of the family unit, my friend, may seem like nothing much to you, but I know the impact personally and have counseled enough girls through the heartbreak of it to know its ability to leave devastating wounds. When families split apart, it makes who you can talk to, be heard by, and connect with challenging. In the best of situations, there are more people to love on you, but in the worst of situations . . . well, you feel divided, and sometimes overlooked. Maybe this type of pain is a part of your story . . . and maybe it's not. Maybe you have a great family. Or maybe your parents are still married, but there are other issues like abuse or addiction or financial troubles or issues with extended family members.

However, the good news is that God is all about redemption. He takes the broken pieces and puts them together to make something incredibly beautiful. Nothing is wasted, even a ripped up shard of glass.

You, my friend, are not beyond God's redemptive work. Nor is your generation. You're not beyond shining beautifully in this world. You're not beyond being used by God to play your part in this world—in your generation—as you tell His story through living your story.

As a matter of fact, I'm pretty sure that God wants to use you to point others to Him as you embrace the unique way He has designed you and find your place in this world.

> *Matthew 5:14-16a MSG*
> *You're here to be light, bringing out the God-colors in the world. God is not a secret to be kept. We're going public with this, as public as a city on a hill. If I make you light-bearers, you don't think I'm going to hide you under a bucket, do you? I'm putting you on a light stand. Now that I've put you there on a hilltop, on a light stand—shine!*

> God designed you to shine
> His light in the places He's put you
> and with the people
> He intends for you to love.

Friend, this little *Mosaic* study is written for you, so that you can discover how to bring your God-color to this world and shine bright in the places that need you most. What's in it for you? Well, when you come to accept yourself and God's work in your life, you'll find the confidence, direction, hope, and purpose you crave. Trust me, that's worth it.

So would you be willing to embrace the process of pursuing God with your questions as you figure out what you believe for yourself? Would you be willing to take the time to explore your God-given wiring, including your strengths and weaknesses, so that you can discover how His power is at work in you? How about uncovering your God-given gifts and discovering ways to love others better? And finally, will you let me give you a little pep talk about facing the hard things in life and a road-map for how to prepare yourself to endure well?

I hope so. I'm praying for you and promise to cheer you on every day we get to spend together in *Mosaic*.

Chapter 1

Own It

embracing your faith

There were at least four conversations going at once—and I'm not sure that is even mathematically logical since there were only seven of us in the car. I was sure the girls would chatter all the way home, based on their energy level as they poured out of the church, and was relieved that they opted to sing instead, with a plea from the back seat to turn up the music. They sang their hearts out, barely stopping to say goodbye as each one jumped out of the van and scurried into their homes on that cool spring night.

As we pulled into the driveway, I detected that something had changed in my oldest daughter's spirit as her sullen expression and scrunched up eyebrows took shape. Her heavy sigh confirmed what I suspected. She quickly declared, "I don't want to go to girls' club anymore."

What? How could that be? Wasn't she singing and laughing with her friends and sister all the way home from church?

"Why not?"

"Because."

"But because why?"

"Nothing."

She sighed again.

We sat there in the stuffy, thick silence until I turned to her little sister, giving her permission to escape and get ready for bed. As I turned to unbuckle, I caught a glimpse of my Leah's eyes welling up and her angry stance diminishing. She fought back her emotions as she raised her voice in frustration.

"Why can't I watch the shows my friends watch? Why can't I listen to the music they listen to? Why do we always have to be . . ."

Be . . .

Leah went on and on about everything in which she felt a source of tension between her friends and family, her world and her faith.

I knew this moment was coming. She was a typical American girl being raised in a Christian home with parents striving to set intentional and grace-filled boundaries, but compared to her friends from her Christian school, we were *that* family with the strictest rules. Seriously, I didn't even want to be *that* family and often wondered how it happened. I totally could identify with how Leah felt — and likely how you feel when your family's rules put you in *that* awkward place with your friends. I may be all grown up, but I still want to fit in, too.

> For the next half hour,
> we sat in the car piecing together
> her feelings like a puzzle that
> had been scattered across a room.

The fun Leah experienced at girls' club was in such contrast to the pressures she felt every single day at school, so her solution was to push her faith and family aside. As we talked, it became apparent that she thought if she could fit in with her classmates by being more like them, then that interal conflict of choosing between faith and friends would stop. Could you blame her for feeling that way?

when you want to quit

Have you ever felt like you wanted to quit your faith or your family? Do you find yourself pleading with your parents to have them change their rules?

Well, you're not alone. Leah wasn't the first nor will she be the last girl to struggle to find acceptance among her friends while honoring her family's rules. I'm not sure, however, if many parents would respond like I did. Do you know what

I said to her? I told Leah she could stop going to girls' club AND she should also quit her faith. Yep, I did that. Right there sitting in the car, I told her to stop considering herself a Christian until she wanted to follow Christ for herself.

I don't know what you think of that solution, but it shocked me, even as the words slipped out of my mouth. See, I knew what it was like to live a life without faith. I was not raised in a Christian home and came to know Jesus as my Savior in college. Living life on both sides has convinced me that life with Jesus is way better than life without out Him. So why would I tell my daughter to quit her faith? Well, because I know the power of choice. See, I got to choose my faith. Well, sort of.

The truth is that God not only chose me, He relentlessly pursued me.

When I finally gave my heart to Jesus, I witnessed such a radical transformation in my life that I was certain God was not a figment of my imagination. The old was gone and the new had come . . .

> *2 Corinthians 5:17 NIV*
> *Therefore, if anyone is in Christ, the new creation has come: The old has gone, the new is here!*

While there have been times I don't understand God or I feel like He is far away from me, I am certain that He is indeed the one true God of the universe and that life with Him is way better than anything I could ask or imagine.

Because I lived without Christ,
I knew the difference of life WITH Christ,
and I didn't ever want it any other way.

But that wasn't Leah's story. She never knew a day without hearing about Jesus. Is that your experience too? Or is your story more like mine? Maybe you don't even know what it means to have a relationship with God.

For Leah, God was as much a part of her story as He could ever be, and to some measure, that made her life *feel* harder. That's why I wanted Leah to choose Jesus for herself. I wanted her to own the decision. I wanted her to be willing to risk the approval of her friends for the sake of knowing Jesus personally, not because she was forced into this life of faith but because she knew in her heart that she was chosen for it!

I want you to choose
your faith as your own, too,
while discovering that
you're already chosen by Him.

Even though I gave Leah permission to quit her faith, I informed her that our family rules wouldn't change regardless of her beliefs. That didn't go over too well, but she agreed to the terms. I also offered her the opportunity to be mentored by me, proposing that we meet once a week and do a little Bible study together. I wasn't trying to convince her that a relationship with Jesus would be worth it, but thought she needed the space to discover for herself if she wanted to be a Christ-follower. Guess what she said? "No. I don't think so." Ugh, my momma heart was crushed, but I masked my reaction with a smile (isn't it amazing how moms can do that?) and told her I loved her no matter what, I promised to pray for her, and, if she changed her mind, I'd be honored to serve her both as mom and mentor (and then I prayed, prayed, and prayed some more).

The next day, Leah greeted me with a smile when she got off the bus (what a relief), and before we were in the door, she said, "Mom, I think I would like you to mentor me after all."

"Oh, really?" I said as I tried to play it cool.

"Yes, really!"

I squealed in delight, before composing myself and re-minding her that she didn't have to do this to please me. It was her choice. HER DECISION. She wanted it, without a doubt, so within a week we began our mother-daughter mentoring time together. We didn't have a clear plan for what to do in our time, but we definitely had a purpose: to help Leah discover if her family's faith would become her own.

The biggest thing we both learned through our time to-gether was how much she needed a safe place to unload the pressures she felt daily while finding a way to embrace her faith as her own. The more pressure Leah felt from friends, the more confused she became and so her knee-jerk reaction was to run away (hmm, makes me think of the story of Jonah!). Have you ever feel this way? Is there something you sense you're supposed to do—specificlly, something consistent with what God says is right and true in the Bible—yet the idea of carrying out the necessary steps feels so scary that you just want to hide? Leah wasn't intentionally following in Jonah's footsteps (Jonah 1:3). She simply didn't know how she'd been chosen by God for a calling unique to her gifts and in line with His purpose for her life.

> *John 15:16 NIV*
> *You did not choose me, but I chose you and appointed you so that you might go and bear fruit—fruit that will last—and so that whatever you ask in my name the Father will give you.*

The pressure Leah felt to fit in with her friends, while still not knowing who she was designed to become, was simply too much. It wasn't until she had time to share her feelings with me that the pressure lifted and she regained her ability to own her decisions and make a plan for how to respond to her friends.

She needed space away from
every opinion to choose the Truth
by which she wanted to live.

Our time together became like oxygen to her, providing her a place to breathe out the world and breathe in the love of Christ as she decided for herself how her faith would define her life.

You need a safe place to breathe, too.

It is one thing for you to be taught by your parents and teachers about matters of faith, but it is another thing to actually believe those truths for yourself. How do I know? Because I've seen this process play out again and again as I've been mentoring teen girls for nearly 20 years, giving them the space to share about the pressures they feel and ask the questions they have about life. One thing I've learned for sure is this:

Teens girls just like you, whether they've been raised in a Christian home or have never heard about Jesus, need processing time to figure out who they are and who they want to become.

It's a choice to own your faith and find your place in God's big world.

You might feel like one little piece of His story and maybe as though you can't make much of a difference, but girl, you are a prized possession of the Most High God. You are a valuable daughter of the King of Kings. You have a place that the God of the Universe has set aside for you to live and breathe and have your being in this world. Isn't it time you discover what that place looks like?

You're one amazing piece in God's mosaic. You have a part to play in His great composition. But it starts with owning exactly where you are at today. Yes, it starts with getting honest with God. So let me set the stage for you and give you some conversation starters — yes, they are starters because I hope you'll embrace having a conversation with God for the rest of your life.

Try It Out

Take a few minutes to read through the questions below to use as a conversation starter with God. If you like to journal, writing out your answers can be a great way to express your feelings.

1. God, right now, I'm feeling . . .
2. God, I wish you would just do this . . .
3. Heavenly Father, if only you would have done . . .
4. Lord, I don't understand why you made me like this . . .
5. God, if I could change anything about myself or my life, I'd like to change . . .

As you open up to talking to God, be willing to hear from Him too. Use this time to surrender to His ways by finishing your conversation time with the prayer below.

Time to Lift Your Voice

Heavenly Father, I am so glad I can come to you honestly and share with you how I'm feeling. Please Lord, I ask you to meet me right where I am too.

Give me your perspective on my life and hope for what you have planned for my future. Help me to not feel alone. Help me to have confidence and courage, that I may live for you without fear of what others may think. Show me how to join you in your work in my life. Show me the areas in which I need to take responsibility and change, and give me the power to do so. Thank you for loving me and choosing me. Help me to choose you all of my days, too. In Jesus's Name, Amen.

Think On This

1. Could you resonate with Leah's story of being pulled in different directions, especially between her parents' rules and what her friends were doing?

2. What would you do if you were given the chance to quit your faith?

3. Would you love to have someone to process life with out loud? If so, what can you do about it? If not, can you think about why this is a hesitation for you?

4. What would you think about asking your mom or an aunt, an older friend, or woman from church to spend some "mentoring" time with you? Maybe going through this study together?

5. How would choosing to live for God change your life today? Is that something you want to think about doing? If so, what could be your first step?

Visit http://moretobe.com/mosaic-resources/ for resources to use throughout this study.

CHAPTER 2

Strong Connection

growing in a relationship with God

I'm wondering, have you ever been compared to a lamp? My guess is likely not, but if you don't mind, I'd like you to consider this simple, yet abstract, illustration as a way of thinking differently about your relationship with God and your purpose in this world.

Let's start with a little observation. If you take a minute to look around your home, how many different types of lamps do you see? Are there tall ones and short ones? How about fancy ones in your living room and functional ones at a desk? As you take the time to consider each one, think about how they all serve a unique purpose—to shine bright in the spot where they have been placed along with adding a bit of personality to the space. Hmm. Sound familiar? Could the same thing be said about you?

> Yes, you are hand picked by God to shine bright in the place He's set aside for you to perfectly light up this world.

Yes, friend, you've been uniquely designed by God to be used in a very specific way in this world, in the same way the lamps in your home and mine have been handpicked to serve a specific purpose. You have a unique personality, spiritual gifts, talents, and passions put together by God to be used in your family, friendships, and community. Maybe you've never thought of your life from this perspective, but what if you did? What if knowing your uniqueness was the secret to bringing your God-color to this world? Could that be a way to shine bright as God's child and become a light to the world?

I'm not the first to compare you to a lamp. God actually does so in Matthew 5. Consider it in the English Standard Version translation instead of The Message, which I shared with you in the introduction:

Matthew 5:14-16 ESV
You are the light of the world. A city set on a hill cannot be hidden. Nor do people light a lamp and put it under a basket, but on a stand, and it gives light to all in the house. In the same way, let your light shine before

others, so that they may see your good works and give glory to your Father who is in heaven.

When God created you, He set you apart to shine in this world for Him (that's what it means to give glory to your Father in heaven). And yet, being called to shine doesn't mean you'll feel like shining or even know how to shine! Maybe you feel more like that light put under a basket, because of all the pressure that is upon you or the fear of not fitting in with your friends. Aren't there moments when you feel so out of place and insecure that you just want to hide, not shine?

So, how do you fulfill this amazing call to shine bright when it feels like you're stuck in the dark?

You start shining by ceasing to try. How could that be the solution? Well, my friend, because you're not supposed to be the one doing the shining, but rather God is wanting to use you as His vessel to shine through. See, it's all about plugging into a relationship with God in which He does all the work to make you shine!

Try It Out

Since we're busy talking about lamps and how unique they are, I have a little assignment for you. Would you mind taking a few minutes to get on the Internet and search for "lamps," then click on the link to view images?

So what do you see? Quite an eclectic collection of lamps, don't you think? As you look at each one, pretend to give each lamp a name and a job—like that pink one might be called Rosie, because she likes to make everyone smile, and that orange-gold one might be Dawn, because she reminds you of the sunrise.

When you're done labeling a few lamps, take a few minutes to think about your friends and family. Consider how each person is unique but also plays an important role in your life. Think also about how you play a significant part in their life, too. Not the same. Definitely different. But certainly needed.

your power source

Have you ever noticed how important it is for lights to be wired correctly? When the wiring is all wonky, it causes quite a problem. For example, in one of my homes, there was a light switch on the wall in our living room that worked the basement outlet where we had the treadmill plugged in. This is obviously not an ideal setup and caused quite a stir when one particular family member, who happens to hate exercise, discovers the switched was accidentally flipped just as she was getting ready to burn some calories.

"TURN on the LIGHT switch!" she would holler in frustration.

"The what?"

"The LIGHT!"

"The WHATTTT?"

"The LIGHT SWITCHHH!"

I wonder if hollering burns more energy than the planned workout?

There's a way things
ought to be done.

A switch ought to work an outlet in the same room. That just makes sense, right? Well, in the same way, God has wired us to shine bright in this world. He doesn't intend for us to simply come up with the power source and shine wherever we want to go. Rather, He has made it so that we would be able to shine by being personally connected to Him through a relationship with His son, Jesus.

God is the power source.
Jesus connects us to the power source.
And we are the lamp that holds His light.

Jesus is like the electrical wiring that connects the light to the electricity. Without Him, the lamp won't shine. Think about it. A lamp is of entirely no use if it is not plugged into the outlet, correct? It's the electricity that gives that lamp its purpose, right?

In the same way a light needs a power source in order to burn bright, we also need a power source in order to shine bright in this world. Jesus is where our light comes from. He makes our connection with God possible. Plugging into a relationship with Him will make our light shine, without any effort on our part at all!

the source

The first time I ever heard about getting plugged into a relationship with Jesus was through friends I met working at summer camp when I was still in high school. Those friends loved me to pieces, but I thought they were a little weird. All this Jesus talk made me uncomfortable. I just didn't get it. Do you feel that way too?

As summer pressed on, I became more curious about the way they lived. In contrast to my friends from school, it seemed like they really enjoyed life even though they didn't do all the crazy things I was doing. There was this one guy who especially grabbed my attention, and not just because he had gorgeous blue eyes. He treated me differently than the other guys and was intentional about living out his faith. He went to church on Sundays (even though his parents didn't make him go), didn't cuss (at all), was kind to everyone (especially little kids), and seemed to forgive easily.

His life was in stark contrast to my life. I was a hot-tempered, easily angered, rule-breaking, college-bound girl searching for happiness in all the wrong places. I was constantly looking for people and things and accomplishments to make me feel good about myself, but good grades and faithful friends were never enough. Invitations to parties and travel opportunities never measured up. The latest, fashionable clothes didn't make me feel better. I was still empty on the inside even though life looked great on the outside. Have you struggled with feeling empty, too?

I didn't know that I had this God-size hole in my heart, which the Lord longed to fill. Turning to God didn't feel like an option, either, because I thought, in order for Him to love me and accept me I'd have to follow all His rules—rules that I was really good at breaking. So I looked elsewhere.

My understanding about God was warped because I didn't know the truth that God already loved me and chose me to be His own, even if I hadn't yet chosen Him. God's love for me wasn't based on my behavior but rather on His character. The Bible tells us in 1 John 4:8 that, "God is love." That's who He is, and that's what He does—He loves us before we even love Him.

> God loves us unconditionally,
> without us having to work for it.

The Bible also says that God loves us so much that He gave His only Son, Jesus, so that everyone who believes in Him will spend eternity in heaven with God.

John 3:16 CEV
God loved the people of this world so much that he
gave his only Son, so that everyone who has faith in
Him will have eternal life and never really die.

Do you know what that means? God wants us to be with
Him forever—through eternity! God's desire is for us to
live this life to the fullest, shining bright for Him, while
knowing the goodness of what comes next . . . seeing Him
face-to-face in heaven. What do you think of that plan, my
friend? I admit, it caught me by surprise when I first heard
it explained.

all it takes is a yes

Now, if you've already read *Journey to Freedom* (the first
study in the Engage series available at moretobe.com), this
story of my "yes" to God will be familiar. So how about
you pretend like we're at a family function, where Aunt
Betsy tells her story again and again? Maybe this time, if
you're willing, you might pick up on something new!

So, there I was, in the middle of a study-abroad semester in
London when Mr. Blue Eyes sent me a Bible to soothe my
grieving heart over the loss of our friend's mother. That cer-
tainly wasn't the answer I was looking for, especially since
I had no idea what to make of the verses he highlighted.
With the Bible in hand, I headed upstairs to find my friend

Susie, who happened to be a pastor's kid on another study-abroad program from a Christian college in Florida. I entered her room and threw the Bible on her bed: "What am I supposed to do with this?" Susie ignored my demand for an answer, as she asked me another question instead: "Do you think you're going to heaven when you die?"

Ahem. I didn't know.

I told her I feared I'd broken too many of God's rules to get into heaven. We sat there quietly for a few minutes before she said, "That's not how God works." Really? She went on to explain that God was willing and able to forgive all my sin (those things we do that go against God's instructions for us), and He only asks us to accept that gift through putting our faith in Jesus Christ as Lord and Savior. She described how Jesus' death on the Cross paid the price for our sin, so we didn't owe God a thing.

What a relief! Don't you think so? The hope of heaven is a lot like a one-way ticket to paradise! It sounded too good to be true! God's love without having to work for it? Heaven forever without having to earn it? No more fear over mess-ups for the rest of my life? I decided it was worth trying out this faith in Jesus thing and so I said yes to God. That was the point at which I began my life plugged into God.

connecting

Saying yes to God doesn't have to be a complicated process

or overwhelming experience. Nor does it have to happen again and again. With God, making the connection with Him through faith in His Son is a one-time event. All you have to do is tell God that you believe in your heart that Jesus is Lord as you acknowledge that His death on the Cross paid the price for your sins. That's how you get plugged into God, which is what the Bible calls "being saved."

> *Romans 10:9 ESV*
> *...because, if you confess with your mouth that Jesus is Lord and believe in your heart that God raised him from the dead, you will be saved.*

Saying yes to God is an action we get to take because God has already set us up to do so. He provided Jesus as the one to make our connection with Him possible. Yet God gives us a choice as to whether we want to have that type of relationship with Him and experience the blessings that He has set apart for us.

> *Ephesians 3:4-6 MSG*
> *Long before he laid down earth's foundations, he had us in mind, had settled on us as the focus of his love... Long, long ago he decided to adopt us into his family through Jesus Christ. (What pleasure he took in planning this!) He wanted us to enter into the celebration of his lavish gift-giving by the hand of his beloved Son.*

One of the greatest blessings that comes with our being connected to God through faith in Jesus Christ is finding out who we are and what we are living for—discovering these truths is how we find our purpose and gain perspective on our lives.

> *Ephesians 1:11-12 MSG*
> *It's in Christ that we find out who we are and what we are living for. Long before we first heard of Christ and got our hopes up, he had his eye on us, had designs on us for glorious living, part of the overall purpose he is working out in everything and everyone.*

In addition to the gift of our faith, God also gives us a personal counselor and guide, known as the Holy Spirit.

> *John 14:26 ESV*
> *But the Helper, the Holy Spirit, whom the Father will send in my name, he will teach you all things and bring to your remembrance all that I have said to you.*

The Holy Spirit is our helper who lives within us to give us an understanding of what the Bible really means along with reminding us to live out God's instructions. As we grow in spiritual maturity, especially as a result of reading the Bible, we'll be able to recognize the Spirit's prompting versus our own desires. This doesn't mean listening to the Spirit will be easy. In the same way we have the ability to turn on and off a lamp, we can shut off the working of the Holy Spirit in our lives, too. The Bible calls this "quenching the spirit" and that comes as a result of our sin (1 Thessalonians 5:19).

We might not want to admit it, but we all sin (Romans

3:23). Yes, all of us! Our sin, or disobedience toward God, breaks our connection with Him, somewhat like a loose wire in a lamp makes the connection not work properly. When our connection with God is affected by sin, it needs to be repaired. That happens through the process of confession and repentance—or more simply put: telling God about our sin and making a u-turn in a brand new direction.

God responds to our 'fessing up and turning around by giving us His mercy, grace, and forgiveness. We might still experience the consequences of our actions; however, when our connection with Him is restored, we'll be able to shine bright again!

connecting with divine power

Connecting with God comes through spending time with Him every day. It is similar to the way you spend time with your friends. You make plans to hang out with them, right? And when you are with them, you don't just stand around and stare at each other. You talk! She says something, and you listen. You say something, and she listens. Maybe you do something together, like listening to music, watching something on TV (or YouTube), or you go somewhere together. In the same way, your connection with God needs an intentional investment of your time.

If you've grown up in a Christian family or church community, you might already know that connecting with God is important. Maybe your mom or mentor refers to her Quiet Time or Devotions to describe when she sets apart time to listen and talk to God. And maybe you think that one day, when you're all grown up, you'll have your own Quiet Time, too.

What if you started a habit of connecting with God on your own now?

You don't have to be an adult to connect with God daily. All you need to do is figure out what works best for you as you consider how to read your Bible, spend time in prayer, and look for ways to worship God every day.

There are a number of different ways to go about reading your Bible—and, thankfully, there really is no wrong way to do it. Your focus shouldn't be on the how, but the when, as making time to read Scripture seems to be a challenge for everyone! The enemy likes to convince us that it can wait until later, when really it is everything else that should wait until later. Why? Because the Bible isn't a rule book, but a love letter from God, offering us instruction and wisdom so that we'll be equipped by God to live in this world every single day.

2 Timothy 3:16-17 NIV
All Scripture is God-breathed and is useful for teaching, rebuking, correcting and training in righteousness, so that the servant of God may be thoroughly equipped for every good work.

God gives us the Word, which the Holy Spirit uses to guide us. When the Word is stored up in our hearts and minds, the Holy Spirit will bring it to our attention to teach us, guide us, and encourage us. The Word is also important because it enables us to get to know God and His character. In times when we might doubt that God really cares, we can remember verses like 1 Peter 5:7, "...he cares for you..." and more easily put our trust in Him.

I know what life is like unplugged from God, and I've experienced a radically transformed life as a result of saying yes to God. While my relationship with God didn't change the circumstances of my life, it did affect my perspective and purpose. Instead of turning to the wrong source to find my worth and identity, I pressed into my relationship with God asking Him to show me where and how He wanted me to shine bright for Him. That's what I want for you!

Will you say yes to being plugged into God through a vibrant, growing faith in Jesus, so that you will shine more brightly and more beautifully in this world?

Try It Out

If you want to have a fully connected relationship with God, you need to make time for Him. Here's a little checklist to help you make a plan that works best for you:

1. Pick a Time

Decide on when to read your Bible:
- As soon as you wake up
- After school
- Before homework
- Right before bed

2. Pick a Path

Decide whether you want to use a Bible reading plan to stay focused or just read a chapter a day:
- One Year Bible
- Plans found at YouVersion.com
- Immersed Bible Plan (http://www.moretobe. com/immersed/)

4. Pick a Prayer Style

Just Talk
Talk to God like you would a friend, any time and anywhere.

ACTS
Use this acronym to guide you through four stages of prayer.
1. Adoration: Share with the Lord what you love about Him.
2. Confession: Tell the Lord about your sins.
3. Thanksgiving: Thank the Lord for His provisions in your life.

4. Supplication: Ask the Lord to meet your needs and desires.

Prayer Journal
A prayer journal can be used to record prayer requests and note the date of answered prayers. You can write in paragraph or list style. Using a prayer journal is one way to stay focused during prayer time, too.

Scripture Prayers
Turn Scripture into a prayer, which you can say out loud or write down. Here's an example using Philippians 4:4-7:

> *Lord God, help me to rejoice in You always. Your word says to Rejoice! I pray I would know the full meaning of rejoicing in You. Lord, You desire for my gentleness to be evident to all, and I praise You, Lord, for making that possible. You, Lord, are near to me. You alone keep me from being anxious about anything, but in everything, by prayer and petition, enable me to come to You with thanksgiving, presenting my requests to You. I continue to pray, Lord, that the peace of God, which transcends all understanding, will guard my heart and my mind in Christ Jesus. In His Name, Amen.*

Time to Lift Your Voice

God, thank you for loving me and wanting to be in a relationship with me. I know that I am a sinner who makes mistakes and will continue to do so in the future. Thank you for sending your Son, Jesus Christ, to die for my sins and make me right with you. Please come into my life, God. Fill that hole in my heart with Your love and presence. Help me Lord to learn what that means and to love you most of all so that I may shine bright for you in this world. In Jesus' Strong Name, Amen.

Think On This

1. What do you think of being compared to a lamp and the need to be plugged into God, with Jesus Christ being the connector?

2. How would you describe your faith in God? Is it plugged in? Switched on? Burning out?

3. How would you like your faith to change as you think of the future?

4. When you think about your friends, would you say they are encouraging you or discouraging you to plug into God?

5. As you look at your part in your friendships,

what do you think is your influence on your friends? Take time to consider what may need to change in your friendships.

Visit http://moretobe.com/mosaic-resources/ for resources to use throughout this study.

CHAPTER 3

Wired Wonderfully

embracing His power

In the same way a lamp requires a combination of wires woven together to connect the light bulb fixture to the source of power, God has wired us in such a way that we might bring His light to every place He's designed for us to shine bright. This special God-wiring combines not only our unique personality but also includes aspects like our spiritual gifting, how we learn, the ways we love, and our bent towards problem-solving and leadership styles. When all these things come together, we can begin to see a picture of how God made us on purpose with a perfect combination of strengths and weaknesses, passions and preferences that are needed in this world.

Trust me, uncovering your wiring is a key to embracing who you are and how you're made, so that's what we're going to do over the next two chapters. Rather than looking at every aspect, however, we're going to focus on personality types and spiritual gifts. That's because these two will give you insight into how to shine your God-color bright in your mosaic generation.

God made you on purpose for a good purpose.

Oh girl, you're made well, even if you feel you're not quite good enough. And you are made for this moment, even if parts of your life feel insanely hard. That conflict or challenge that makes you question God and want to quit your faith, and sometimes even life, is really evidence of being an imperfect human who needs an awesome God to fill in your gaps and make His power known in your times of weakness.

Oh yes, you ain't perfect, girlfriend, and you never will be.

Life will always be marked by challenges and trouble, but none that you can't overcome with the power of God at work in you. I'm not saying it will be easy. I'm not saying you'll emerge without bruises and scrapes. But I am saying that this idea that you should be able to keep it all together and be everything to all people is a lie from the devil himself. You will face challenges that impact you personally and play upon the strengths and weaknesses that God has wired together in you.

Conflict Sparks the Wires

Maybe you don't feel like you have any strengths or weaknesses. Maybe you even think your wiring is faulty because you can't figure out how to handle ordinary life problems. Well, friend, your strengths and weaknesses are at work all the time, whether you are aware of them or not. For example, there was a time that my daughter and I had a little "run in" over something that should have been nothing.

I could tell by the look in her eyes that she was incredibly frustrated with me, especially as she let out a huff and held back a snarky comment forming on her lips. You'd think we were going to battle over a dating issue or an unreasonable curfew. Oh no. It wasn't that big of a deal.

Have you been in a tense situation recently with your mom or dad, wondering, "Why are we fighting over this?" There's nothing like conflict to make you feel like you're not good enough and question your God-given purpose.

The conflict with my daughter was over piano playing. Yes, playing, not practicing, as she was not taking lessons. She was innocently passing time trying to teach herself to play one of her favorite songs. I, however, thought I could help her along by giving her some advice. That's all it took to find ourselves in conflict . . . and the sparks in our wiring started to fly.

Our conflict was spurred on by the fact that our ways are different — not wrong — just different because of our God-given personalities.

47

My daughter likes to teach herself everything. She's passionate about conquering a challenge, but only if she can do it her way. Her determination is truly a gift, but can also become a weakness if it turns into a stubbornness that keeps her from receiving instruction from others. Does that sound like you? Or maybe you're more like me. I like to help people solve their problems, which can be a real blessing to those who want to be helped. However, when someone refuses my help, I grow increasingly frustrated, and that's a character weakness that usually leads to conflict.

It certainly would be nice to eliminate our weaknesses, wouldn't it? Then we could live without conflict or feeling bad about ourselves. But when God made us, He made ALL of who we are — strengths and weaknesses combined. He made us fearfully and wonderfully, without mistake.

Psalm 139:14 NIV
I praise you because I am fearfully and wonderfully
made; your works are wonderful, I know that full well.

Unfortunately, seeing the wonderfully-made within you often gets "lost in the sauce." Instead of recognizing the good parts of our wiring, we focus on our short-comings and weaknesses, and that's why we end up feeling like we're not good enough. However, through looking at the different personality types, which each include a distinct set of strengths and weaknesses, we can begin to see how God has wired us together as a whole and complete package. Although we'd like to kick our weaknesses to the curb, God has another plan for them. He didn't make only the parts of our personality that we like — our strengths. He also made the parts that He plans to work through — our weaknesses.

> *2 Corinthians 12:9 NIV*
> *But he said to me, "My grace is sufficient for you, for my power is made perfect in weakness." Therefore I will boast all the more gladly about my weaknesses, so that Christ's power may rest on me.*

As you pinpoint your personality, you can embrace all that is good in the way God has made you, while also surrendering your weaknesses, so that God can use you more powerfully to impact this world.

By giving your weaknesses over to God, He is able to display Christ's strength in you and through you for others to see.

It's like putting a candle in the middle of a broken clay pot—oh my, how the light shines through the cracks. That's how God takes something that is seemingly broken and makes beauty in His own creative way.

you've got personality

Discovering your God-given personality can be a life-changing experience, not only as you see ways to yield your weaknesses to God but also as you come to see things about yourself in a way that finally makes sense. For example, did you know that being shy or talkative or adventurous or organized are all character traits of different personalities? That's why everyone in the same family won't enjoy the same things, even if they have all been exposed to the identical experiences and opportunities.

So how do you figure out your personality and truly embrace the way God made you...strengths...weaknesses... and everything in between? Psychologists have come up with hundreds of different assessments for pinpointing personality types. Some personality tests help you identify skill sets, passions, and career paths. Other assessments focus more on relationship skills and temperaments, such as the one that categorize personalities based on the work done by the Greek physician, Hippocrates, thousands of years ago. He divided the temperaments into four categories, Sanguine, Choleric, Melancholy, and Phlegmatic, which look like this:

Susie **Sanguine** is a social butterfly, who is loud, bubbly, super friendly, but is often forgetful, trivia obsessed, and annoyingly happy at times.

Clara **Choleric** is the leader and problem-solver who can get things done, but she can also be on the bossy side, easily angered, and unsympathetic.

Maggie **Melancholy** is more of the sensitive and artistic or theatrical type who has a careful eye for detail and likes everything in order, but can be bit of a pessimist who gets easily depressed.

Paige **Phlegmatic** is a laid-back observer who prefers to hang out behind the scenes, often procrastinating while avoiding conflict and finding a way out of making any decision.

Personality types include a combination of strengths and weaknesses, which look something like this:

Sanguine

Strengths	*Weaknesses*
Lively	Too Happy For Some
Social	Hates to Be Alone
Confident	Not Organized
Story Teller	Wastes Time Talking
Teachable	Undisciplined

Choleric

Strengths	*Weaknesses*
Excels in Emergencies	Impulsive
Seeks Practical Solutions	Demanding
Can Run Anything	Controlling
Born Leader	Outspoken
Sees the Whole Picture	Impatient

Melancholy

Strengths	*Weaknesses*
Detailed	Rigid
Artistic/Musical	Moody
Organized	Too High Standard
Idealistic	Highly Critical
Independent	Holds Back Affection

Phlegmatic

Strengths	*Weaknesses*
Adaptive	Indifferent to Plans
Diplomatic	Too Compromising
Steady	Not Goal-Oriented
Consistent Life	Dislikes Change
Compassionate	Judges Others

When we pinpoint our personality type, we can look at how the combination of strengths and weaknesses go together. This is what enables us to embrace our strengths while also giving a clear picture of the weaknesses that need our attention. As we consider the personality types, we'll also be able to recognize how others are wired, and then can respond in a more compassionate way…which will lead to less conflict!

For example, when my daughter resisted my help at the piano, I became frustrated until I remembered that I was coming across as bossy to her. I forgot that I needed to ask if she wanted help before stepping in. When I recognized this was part of the issue, I backed off and gave her space to play and learn on her own. She was also working on her weaknesses, too. Instead of snapping at me, her "huff" was an attempt to be not so easily irritated, knowing I was only trying to help. Keeping each other's personalities in mind, as we embrace our own unique type, minimizes our conflict and enables us to back out of ugly situations more easily!

When our weaknesses dominate our personalities, we might find ourselves in a mess with others and even with God. But through humbling ourselves before the Lord, we can enable Him to work in our mess and use our uniquely designed personality to shine bright for Him.

When we are weak, others have the potential of seeing more of God at work.

For example, Miss Clara Choleric may find herself being a little too bossy in a leadership moment while Miss Paige Phlegmatic may not say a word in order to avoid conflict. In both of those cases, their strengths—leadership and peacemaking—have gone to the extreme and have become their weaknesses. The solution for both is the same:

- slow down and ask God to work through them
- seek forgiveness from God and those they've hurt
- ask God to work through their weakness

Remember, we all have weaknesses, so don't think yours are the worst. They're just different and need to be yielded to God in order to keep them in check. God didn't make a mistake when He made you.

We all have strengths and weaknesses within our personalities, and we'll often find ourselves attracted to the strengths we see in others that we find as weaknesses in ourselves

Learning about the different personalities can help you understand how to better relate to people, too. By identifying what you like in others, you can also choose to "put up" with their weaknesses a little bit more graciously, especially when you understand that what you're experiencing is a "packaged deal." Imagine how that would impact your friendships and even family interactions!

So how about taking some time to determine your personality type? It's worth the exploration! Trust me!

Try It Out

There are a number of ways to determine your personality type, with a number of options available online for free:

- http://www.41q.com/
- http://www.123test.com/disc-personality-test/

As you look at the results of your scores, keep these two principles in mind:

Age
You're still maturing, so some of the questions may not relate to your life experience as of yet. The more you live, the more your personality will take shape, so feel free to hold the results loosely while also being willing to take the assessment again in the future.

Masking

There is a possibility you may have a masked score, which means your God-given personality has been significantly influenced by a strong personality type of someone else in your life, such as a parent, teacher, or coach. In other words, you've adopted their way of thinking and functioning.

It could also be the result of having experienced a trauma or being in a dysfunctional environment impacted by an addiction or some kind of abuse. If your score is masked, you'll notice a sense of conflict in your feeling of what the assessment should say about you and what you feel about yourself. Feel free to take the assessment again, now and in the future, and ask a loving adult to walk through it with you.

Going Deeper

If you love this idea of discovering your personality type and are going through this process with your parent, you may want to consider a more in-depth exploration that can be a great tool for assessing college and career focus. The Highlands Battery looks at personality type along with leadership type, learning style, gifts and talents, and offers clear direction for the best fit for study environments, college majors, and career choices.

If you'd like to learn more about this study, ask your mom, dad, or guardian to contact me about

The Highlands Battery and make sure they mention you learned about it in Mosaic so that I can offer you a discount on the assessment fee. You can learn more about it here: http://www.elisapulliam.com/highlands/.

Time to Lift Your Voice

Lord God, thank you for wiring me exactly how you designed. Please, God, show me how to embrace my strengths and weaknesses, that you may accomplish your purposes in me. Show me how the sparks of conflict are really evidence of the way you made each of us unique and rather than fearing those moments, yielding to you in them. In Jesus' Name, Amen.

Think On This

1. What do you think are your God-given strengths?

2. How can you use them in a positive way to bless your family, encourage your friends, or serve in your school?

3. What are your God-given weaknesses?

4. How can you go about surrendering them to the

Lord so that His power may work through you?

**Visit http://moretobe.com/mosaic-resources/
for resources to use throughout this study.**

CHAPTER 4

Gifted
for Love

appointed for your part

While discovering personalities can be a wonderful way
to find your God-color, it's only one part of your complete
package. God also has appointed a distinct spiritual gift for
you to use and enjoy. Now, a spiritual gift is not like a big
present that shows up on Christmas morning. We don't get
to ask for it nor do we have to wait to open it up. A spiritual
gift isn't something we can trade in for another gift, either.
There is no return policy on spiritual gifts. A spiritual gift
is just that—a gift from God to be used to bless our broth-
ers and sisters in the family of God. It is bestowed on us by
God for the sake of using it to serve others:

1 Peter 4:10
Each one should use whatever gift [she] has received to
serve others...

The Scriptures also tell us that the gift we've been given is
distributed by God to show people all about God:

1 Corinthians 12:4-11 MSG
God's various gifts are handed out everywhere; but they
all originate in God's Spirit. God's various ministries
are carried out everywhere; but they all originate in
God's Spirit. God's various expressions of power are
in action everywhere; but God himself is behind it all.
Each person is given something to do that shows who
God is: Everyone gets in on it, everyone benefits. All
kinds of things are handed out by the Spirit, and to all
kinds of people! The variety is wonderful: wise coun-
sel, clear understanding, simple trust, healing the sick,
miraculous acts, proclamation....
All these gifts have a common origin, but are hand-
ed out one by one by the one Spirit of God.
He decides who gets what, and when.

So what exactly are the spiritual gifts? And how do we
know which one God has given us? Well, the theologians
(the people who study God's Word) have come up with
quite an extensive list of gifts as well as descriptions for
how they are used in the body of Christ. I know that some
of the terms may seem strange to you, so I've given each
gift a "role" describing how you might see a person using
that particular gift. You'll also find a description of what

each gift looks like and where it is found in the Bible.

Messenger
Evangelism - Eph. 4:11
Enjoys telling others about the Bible and Jesus.

Planner or Administrator
Administration - 1 Cor. 12:28
Likes to work toward God-given goals through planning, organizing, and supervising.

Missionary
Apostle - Eph. 4:11; 1 Cor. 12:28
Desires to be sent forth to new places with the Gospel.

Counselor
Discernment & Prophecy - 1 Cor. 12:10, Rom. 12:6, Eph. 4:11
Has a clear sense whether the behavior or teaching is from God, Satan, human error, or human power and/or tells others about God's message.

Sunday School or Bible Teacher
Teaching - Rom. 12:7; 1 Cor. 12:28, Eph. 4:11
Enjoys instructing others in the Bible in order to help people grow in their faith.

Leader
Leadership - Rom. 12:8
Desires to lead and motivate others to get involved in the accomplishment of God's goals.

Bible Student

Knowledge - 1 Cor. 12:8

Enjoys learning as much as possible about the Bible.

Encourager

Exhortation & Faith - Rom. 12:8, 1 Cor. 12:8-10

Comes alongside of someone with words of encouragement and counsel to help others be all God wants them to be and/or has an extraordinary belief in God's power.

Giver

Giving - Rom. 12:8

Shares their resources with cheerfulness without requiring a promise of return.

Prayer Warrior

Healing & Prayer - 1 Cor. 12:9, 28, 30

Uses prayer and acts of service to bring about God's healing.

Servant

Mercy & Service - 1 Cor. 12:28, Rom 12:7-8

Serves through meeting needs and by responding with sensitivity to those in difficult situations.

Hostess

Hospitality - 1 Pet. 4:9,10

Serves by warmly welcoming people, even strangers, into their home or church and providing food or lodging.

Pastor

Pastor & Shepherd - Eph. 4:11
Feels responsible for protecting, guiding, and feeding a group of believers entrusted to their care.

After reading through this list, you might be thinking, "I have no idea what my spiritual gift is!" Well, that's totally okay. These gifts become obvious as you mature, although some may stand out from an early age. You can experiment with serving your family, friends, and church in lots of different ways to see if you can pinpoint your spiritual gift. When you get that feeling of "I just love to do this" and a sense of never tiring of the task, you'll know that's your spiritual gift at work. God will no doubt provide you with opportunities to use your spiritual gift, because that is His is purpose, so don't worry over what it is. Rather, choose to enjoy the adventure of discovering your spiritual gift by serving the people God has put in your life!

Try It Out

I'd certainly love for you to figure out your spiritual gift and to begin using it now to bless others. Take the time to read through the Spiritual Gifts list and discuss it with your mom or a mentor. Consider what opportunities exist for you to "try out" the gifts within your church or in your family. You may also want to do an online assessment such as http://www.churchgrowth.org/cgi-cg/gifts.cgi?intro=1.

A spiritual gift is really a means to express God's love to others. What a privilege, really! But just because you have a gift and desire to use it to love others well doesn't mean it will come naturally or manifest itself the way you see gifts working out in others. That's because the way you like to express love and receive love is unique to your God-given wiring. Let me explain.

you've got a love language

Have you ever considered that you have a particular love language? A love language is the way you are naturally bent towards receiving and giving love. According to Dr. Gary Chapman, there are five common love languages:

1. Words of Affirmation
2. Acts of Service
3. Receiving Gifts
4. Quality Time
5. Physical Touch

Dr. Chapman explains in his book, *The Five Love Languages*, that each of us have this deeply felt need to experience love in a unique way. When we receive "our style of love," we actually feel like a happy hot air balloon floating through the blue summer sky. But when our love tank is empty, it may feel like a great airplane flew right into our balloon. Pop. Gone are the feelings of security and connection.

To be loved is to be known.

We're designed by God to be loved, and yet human love will never match God's love for us. We've also been duped into believing that love is a feeling, when by God's design, it is most definitely an action.

Love is a verb. Not a noun.

Oh, sure, we love to use the word *love* to describe our emotions or passions. We love chocolate ice cream and playing basketball. We love our best friends and families. We love a TV show and a music group. We love Jesus. But are we really, truly loving all these things and people equally?

Unfortunately, our English language uses the word love to describe things we enjoy as well as those people (and sometimes things) we truly love without offering a way to clarify the depth of our feelings. Maybe this is why we forget that love is more than a feeling—it is an emotion that requires a physical response.

Try It Out

It's hard to feel God's love when things are not going well. That's why we need to have the truth stored up in our hearts and minds. Take a few minutes to soak in the truth about God's love:

1. **Search for Love**: Go to Biblegateway.com and

search for "love." Isn't it amazing how many verses there are? Browse through them and take time to read some within the context of the chapters. Talk about what those verses tell you about God's love for you and the ways you can love Him, too.

2. **Pick 2 Verses:** Pick two verses that stand out the most to you. Write them on index cards, or, if you want to get crafty, make them pretty and put them in picture frames!

3. **Memorize Love:** Set a goal for memorizing those two verses and plan a reward, like making those double chocolate cupcakes.

If we look at what the Bible has to say about love—in particular, loving others—we find plenty of insight. For example, 1 Corinthians 13 describes love as a sacrificial, never-ending gift. Love is not prideful and always giving. In Colossians 3:12, we discover we've been chosen for love and yet it is something we must put on:

Colossians 3:12-14 MSG
So, chosen by God for this new life of love, dress in the wardrobe God picked out for you: compassion, kindness, humility, quiet strength, discipline. Be even-tempered, content with second place, quick to forgive an offense. Forgive as quickly and completely as the Master forgave you. And regardless of what else you put on, wear love. It's your basic, all-purpose garment. Never be without it.

Love is the foundation of our wardrobe,
picked out personally by God.

What does it look like to put on a God-colored, love-marked wardrobe? Well, instead of focusing on what you want from people, you can look for ways to love others more purposefully while also guarding yourself against seeking love in all the wrong places. Oh yes, I'm sure you know that temptation to seek others to fill that God-size hole in your heart instead of giving God that emptiness. You have to be careful who you expect to receive love from and what you're willing to accept from others through guarding your heart:

> *Proverbs 4:23*
> *Above all else, guard your heart, for everything you do flows from it.*

Whatever takes up residence in your heart will flow throughout your life, so you've got to be very careful about who you turn to in order to have your love tank filled up. Don't follow in my footsteps! I was like an empty cup walking around from guy to guy, willing for them to fill me up with anything, even if it was totally not good for me.

That refreshing and filling love you
crave comes from Jesus above all else!

Yes, we can be loved well by others, but not like how we're loved by Jesus. Certainly, someone who loves Jesus first may be able to love us from that overflow, right? Even so, no one can replace God. That's why it's so important to consider your heart motive when it comes to this matter of love as well as where the other person is coming from. You can seek the Lord for His wisdom as you consider these questions:

Does this person appear to have a relationship with God, and in particular, believe in Jesus as their Lord?

Is this person seeking to live according to what the Bible says is true?

Are they using me to fill up their love tank?

Am I tempted to use this person to fill up my tank?

Are we encouraging each other to seek God for all our needs and loving others as an overflow of our relationship with Him?

As you use these questions to discern the health of your relationships, with friends and even in a dating situation, you'll be able to we pinpoint whether you're putting on the wardrobe of love and more intentionally be able to use your spiritual gift and express love according to your natural bent. You'll also be more conscious of your tendency to seek love from the wrong places. For example, if your love language is touch, you might find yourself being too affectionate with guys at school (do your friends tell you you're flirting?), even though you don't mean anything by it. If that's the case, you may need to set a policy for yourself like "no hugging guys." Yet, knowing you have this need for touch, you may want to grab your little sister and read a book with her, or snuggle with your mom while watching a TV show. You need touch, because God made you that way, but you've got to guard against the wrong type of touch. The same goes for all of us with our different types of love languages, needs, and desires.

> God made us to love others
> as an expression of His love.

John 13:34-35 couldn't make this any plainer.

> *John 13:34-35 NIV*
> *A new command I give you: Love one another. As I have loved you, so you must love one another. By this everyone will know that you are my disciples, if you love one another*

By identifying the way you are most comfortable giving the gift of love, you'll find new opportunities to show the love of Christ to people who God has set apart for you to bless. As you grow in your understanding of the love languages, you'll also be able to recognize opportunities to step beyond your comfort zone and love others in response to His love for you.

Try It Out

Would you like to figure out your love language? It is so simple! Go online to complete an assessment at http://www.5lovelanguages.com/profile/.

Be thoughtful about the results, especially considering how to guard yourself from getting false love in the wrong places. Take time to brainstorm ways to love others better through discovering your family member's and friend's love languages, too.

Remember, my friend, you are uniquely created by God. Your personality, spiritual gifts, and love language are perfectly put together by the Lord, designed for you to be used for Him and by Him in this world. It is my prayer for you to embrace your God-given uniqueness—for that is what it means to embrace your God-color and discover your purpose in shining bright and beautiful for Him.

Time to Lift Your Voice

Lord God, thank you for giving me a spiritual gift to be used for the sake of encouraging and helping those belonging to your family. Thank you also for the ways you have made me to show your love and receive it. Enable me to love those you've brought into my life the way they need to be loved. Help me to be after your love most of all, and not seek a counterfeit in any way. In Jesus's Name, Amen.

Think On This

1. What do you think your spiritual gift may be? How can you positively use it?

2. What are the ways you like to be shown love? What ways do you like to give love?

3. How can you use your love language in a positive way? What do you need to be careful of?

4. Looking at yourself as a whole package, how do you think God wants to use you to shine bright in this world?

Visit http://moretobe.com/mosaic-resources/ for resources to use throughout this study.

CHAPTER 5

Beyond the Why

pressing on with purpose

Are you starting to see what your God-color might look like? Have you gotten a glimpse of the way God wants to use your personality style, strengths and weaknesses, spiritual gifting, and love language? All these pieces, and more, are glimmers into seeing how God wants you to shine bright for Him in this world. And yet, my friend, there's a tough topic we must tackle before you can launch forward with a greater sense of purpose.

Have you ever wondered why life is so stinking hard at

times?

Well, I have a secret to tell you.

Life is hard. Always and often. But it doesn't have to be without hope.

That's not really a secret. God tells us that life will be hard, but for some reason we like to overlook those verses.

> *Matthew 6:34 NIV*
> *Therefore do not worry about tomorrow, for tomorrow will worry about itself. Each day has enough trouble of its own.*

He also tells us that in Him we can find our hope.

> *Romans 15:13*
> *May the God of hope fill you with all joy and peace as you trust in him, so that you may overflow with hope by the power of the Holy Spirit.*

While small things, like a pimple on the end of your nose on the day of class pictures, might just make you cranky, they will eventually pass. That sort of hard is temporary. But there are an infinite number of bigger issues that seek to steal your joy, rob your hope, deflate your sense of purpose, and leave you feeling like you've got nothing left to live for. That trial may come in the form of your family busting apart in the wake of your parents' divorce or finding out that you have to move because your dad got a new job. Hard like that ain't gonna go away. So how can you move through challenging times without losing perspective on your life purpose and being willing to shine your God-color in this world?

When you're the emotional type, like me, it is a challenge to not let your feelings dominate your thinking. I'm often tempted to turn away from God when I feel like the "bad" could be my fault. That's my default reaction, as I doubt God's love and wonder if I somehow made Him upset. And that's exactly how I felt one summer when I ended up sick in bed a week before we were supposed to go camping. As though the illness wasn't bad enough, in a span of three days the water was accidently shut off to our house, my computer died while working on a big project, I had a fight with a family member, and my friend's dad died in a tragic accident two days before we were supposed to leave on the long-awaited trip with them. It was an awful series of events, to say the least.

We prayed and talked as a family, and finally decided to continue ahead with our plans to camp at another location, in spite of the prediction for rain. By the time we arrived at the campground, the dark clouds were gathering overhead. We raced between the raindrops pitching the tent and securing the tarp to the trees with ropes. As my husband tied the last knot, the skies opened up. The rain poured down buckets, hitting the ground so fast it created mini-rivers through the gravel underneath the tent, lifting it off the ground. The girls dug gullies around the tent to redirect the water toward the hill below, while I grabbed the twins and ran for cover under Nana's cabin porch 100 yards away.

I didn't know if I should laugh or cry
as I begged God for an answer,
"Why, God? Why?"

When the bad bombards our lives, we usually end up crying out to God, wanting to know why. As though the answer to the "why" question would change our circumstances! It never does. But what can we do in that moment, when we must press on in spite of the mess?

but why?

It is impossible to know the mind of God (1 Corinthians 2:16 NLT). With the passing of time, we may be able to see the reason, but in the middle of it all, searching for why can leave us hopeless.

I was certainly feeling hopeless in the middle of that down-pour while trying to set up our campsite, wondering what on earth we'd do in the lake that was once our dry piece of ground as I looked on from the covered porch of my mother-in-law's cabin. Just as I was dreaming of blue skies, a loud crack snapped me back to reality. A tree limb above our site split off and fell from 40 feet high. We gasped as we thought it was going to hit the camper in the site next to our tent, but there was no sound. It was dead quiet, until we heard our oldest daughter scream: "She's been hit." I took off like an Olympic runner, sprinting across the mud crying out "Jesus. Jesus. Jesus!"

I feared that our middle daughter had been knocked unconscious, or worse, dead. I know that might seem a bit dramatic, but I couldn't see her from behind the tent and never heard her cry out. By the time I reached the site, her daddy had her in his arms, blood running down her face. The tree limb—about 15 feet long and at least three inches thick—hit the highest part of her cheek and just above her eye. She let out a sobbing cry before falling into shock.

"Oh God, WHY?"

We carried Abby over to the cabin, grabbing ice from the cooler as we tried to figure out what to do next. Fortunately, there was a hospital nearby, so we headed into town to have her checked out. I stood outside the MRI room begging God, "Please, let her be okay. Please, God. Please God." I was terrified of the outcome, and how I'd react. I knew that God's plans were bigger than mine, and I was keenly aware of the fact that His intentions for how to use this situation might not line up with my desires. I cried out to Him:

> *God, I am so mad right now. After this no-good-very-bad-totally-unhappy last ten days, why does this have to happen? I know you won't tell me why, but at least tell me what to do, because right now I want to quit You forever even though I know how much I need You. Please help me, God, to see you at work and to trust you more than what I feel at the moment. In Jesus' Name Amen.*

As Abby began to come out of the shock, we learned from the doctors that there was no fracture or internal bleeding nor any damage to her eye. We were discharged from the hospital with instructions to care for her mild concussion and were advised to put off our plans to go to the amusement park for at least another day. Deflated but relieved, we made a detour by Dairy Queen (because ice cream always makes a bad moment better) on the way home. In the secret parts of my heart and mind, I wrestled again with God. Looking at Abby's beat-up face, I couldn't find a single answer as to why God would allow this to happen. I continued to pray, wanting some sort of perspective change, so that my hurt wouldn't turn to anger and bitterness.

> I could be mad at God
> and pull away from Him,
> or I could draw near
> to God and thank Him.

Yes, thank Him, even in the middle of the mess. I decided I'd rather be nearer to God in a mess than far from God and alone. So I started thanking God for everything that came to mind and urged my family to do the same:

Thank you God for sparing Abby from greater harm and for literally saving her life.

Thank you God for a hospital being nearby and the provision of medical insurance (these are the things that moms think of as they are signing the hospital paperwork).

Thank you God for the way you are at work in a way we have yet to even see.

Thank you God that we can find our hope in You even when things don't make sense at all.

As I thanked God, my stinkin' thinkin' changed from focusing on the WHY question to embracing the truth—the truth that God's provision and love for us can't be measured by our circumstances.

God's love for us never changes, never gives up, and never ends.

God's love is steadfast—that means steady on or stayed on. *Steady and staying.* His love for us doesn't move or change, even when we move away from Him in the middle of an emotional hissy-fit. (Yes, that's what I was having during the rainstorm.) The mess we find ourselves in, while sometimes a result of our own foolishness or sin, can also be the result of living in a broken and imperfect world. We can't equate our trouble with a lack of God's love for us. However, in our trouble, we need to remind ourselves that God's love for us is never ending!

> *Psalm 100:5 NIV*
> *For the LORD is good and his love endures forever;*
> *his faithfulness continues through all generations.*

It is in the tough times that God wants us to press on through the difficulty, as we cling to His truth and find comfort in His love for us. But how? Read on. I'll tell you how.

choose truth and do the "hupo"

God allows trouble to come our way, not because He likes to see us suffer but because He has a greater plan at work. Because we belong to God through faith in Jesus Christ, we can know for certain that He has good in store for us. His promise in Romans 8:28 stands true, regardless of what the enemy hopes to accomplish.

Romans 8:28 NIV
And we know that in all things God works for the good of those who love him, who have been called according to his purpose.

The problem is that our definition of good and God's definition of good are often different. Good doesn't always mean happy, easy, or comfortable.

God's good can mean being changed from the inside out to be more like Christ.

His good may mean we have to walk through trial and suffering, as He not only changes our lives on the inside but also uses our story to draw others to Him. His good can be all about using an ugly situation to cause a person to see Jesus for the first time and choose to accept Him as their Savior.

While God is at work accomplishing His good in our lives

with an eternal purpose in mind, the enemy of God, Satan, is at work attempting to knock that plan off-course. The devil is on a mission to steal, kill, and destroy us, even though God has plans for us to have a full life.

> *John 10:10 NIV*
> *The thief comes only to steal and kill and destroy; I have come that they may have life, and have it to the full.*

Satan is always positioning himself to attack us and wear us down (Daniel 7:25 KJV). The attack may be a series of little issues that leave us feeling overwhelmed and defeated. Or Satan may be tormenting us in our everyday thoughts and emotions, leading us to feel sad or ashamed. Yes, you can blame Satan for stinkin' thinkin'. He may also worm his way into a huge issue—like disease, divorce, or death—causing us to fear the future and feel unable to press on.

> If God's desire is for His light
> to shine bright in us,
> then of course the enemy is
> going to try to snuff us out.

Satan beats us down, causing our faith to flicker like a light right before the bulb burns out. That flickering needs to be our warning sign to tell Satan to take a hike! It's okay to give the devil some attitude as you stand on the truth that the victory belongs to Christ alone. That's exactly what Jesus did when he saw Satan at work in Peter's life.

Matthew 16:23
Get behind me, Satan! You are a hindrance to me. For
you are not setting your mind on the things of God, but
on the things of man.

We need to tell Satan to buzz off when he feeds us lies
about who God is, what God does, and who we are as children of God. While we may not be able to pin our troubles
entirely on Satan—because we need to take responsibility
for our actions knowing that sometimes our trouble is a
result of our disobedience or foolishness—we need to be
aware that Satan will tempt us to wrestle against God and
pull back from Him. It is in times of trouble that we need to
press on in faith and lean into God, instead of running from
Him.

Remember how my response to the tree-limb-falling fiasco
left me questioning God and feeling totally defeated? Yet
as I walked through the shock of the whole experience, I
turned to the Lord and asked Him for a new perspective.
That process was something I learned how to do a few
summers earlier when I heard a pastor speak on the topic of
perseverance and suffering. Oh, fun, right? Well, I wasn't
thrilled to spend a week listening to this guy preach on the
matter of trouble, but it has turned out to be one of those
truths I wish someone would have taught me when I was
younger!

News Alert: We will all have trouble.

It doesn't matter if we have been Christians since birth

or are brand new to the faith, ALL of us will face trouble, because that's what the Bible promises will happen. So can you think of at least one bit of trouble in your life right now, no matter how big or small it may seem? Maybe it is getting cut from the play because you couldn't sing good enough? Or maybe your family is going through a medical crisis? Yes, I personally know what all these things feel like—trouble! Some of this trouble may make you cry for a few days while the other circumstances can cause you to shed tears for years.

So if we're promised a life with trouble, what should we do about it? Well, we can actually stop asking the "why" question and move onto the "what." In other words, we need to learn how to live in spite of the trouble. For many of us, that means a new way of thinking and living. It means learning how to do the "hupo." Yes, hupo, not to be confused with hippo.

Hupo is the nickname I've come up with for a fancy Greek word known as *Hupomone*. (Did you know that the Old Testament in the Bible was written in Hebrew and the New Testament is written in Greek and Aramaic? That means we can sometimes get a better understanding of the meaning of an English word in the Bible when we look at the original language.) *Hupomone* is the Greek word for perseverance, as it is used in James:

> *James 1:2-4 NIV*
> *. . .whenever you face trials of many kind . . . know that the testing of your faith produces perseverance. Let perseverance finish its work so that you may be mature*

and complete, not lacking anything.

Maybe the Message translation will make more sense to you:

> *James 1:2-4 MSG*
> *Consider it a sheer gift, friends, when tests and challenges come at you from all sides. You know that under pressure, your faith-life is forced into the open and shows its true colors. So don't try to get out of anything prematurely. Let it do its work so you become mature and well-developed, not deficient in any way.*

Perseverance—or *hupomone*—means "a person who is not swerved from their faith...even in the greatest trials and sufferings." In other words, perseverance describes how to face trouble. It is a call for us to press on in our faith during times of suffering and trouble. When we do that, we'll find unexpected blessing in the form of spiritual growth and unquenchable joy. Even in the midst of trouble—like when a storm floods your campsite and a tree limb falls from above—you can still find joy as you press on in your faith.

Doing the hupo—persevering—turns trouble into an opportunity to experience God's faithfulness while we practice being faith in return. It is a chance to show the enemy who's really Boss! Instead of running from the trial, we turn and run into it with our hands raised up in a position of surrender. We stop asking that universal question "Why me?" and instead ask...

> God, what do you want me
> to learn through this and
> how can I give
> glory in my response?

As we do the hupo, we shift our "why" question about trouble into a "what now" response as we fight against the enemy's attempt to totally disconnect us from God. Instead of succumbing to lies, we do exactly what is outlined for us in James 4:

> *James 4:7-8 NIV*
> **Submit** *yourselves, then, to God.*
> **Resist** *the devil, and he will flee from you.*
> **Come** *near to God and he will come near to you.*

Could responding to trials with unwavering faith be any simpler? It may be plain, but it's still challenging to put this Word into practice:

1. **Submit to God!**
   Raise up your hands in surrender, not asking why, but what.

2. **Resist the Devil!**
   Tell Satan to take a hike!

3. **Come Near to God!**
   Run straight into God's protective love and covering of grace.

That's what doing the hupo looks like, as we choose to face our troubles and press on in our faith in the Lord. It may seem easy, but in times of trouble it takes discipline to walk by faith through those three steps. It also takes a habit of connecting with God, so that running to Him doesn't seem strange. That's why we started this study with deciding how to own your faith by making time to be in the Word daily and talking with the Lord. Those convo times with God are necessary for developing the type of connected relationship with Him that you'll need when life's ugliness comes your way.

Try It Out

Trouble is an opportunity for our faith to grow and for God to get the glory. To see how one amazing young woman has pressed on in her life of trouble, watch this video of para-olympian Stef Reid: https://youtu.be/XXpbQi5ESSQ.

As you think about her story, consider how you'd respond if you were her, and what it would take for you to have that type of faith and perseverance.

Maybe you've been through so much that Stef's story doesn't seem that big of a deal. Maybe you've not experienced any sort of suffering in your life. Either way, my friend, the point is not to compare. It's to learn. It's to look around and see how those who say they love God walk in faith through the tough stuff--and then make a mental note to follow in their footsteps should the Lord give you the op-

portunity to do the hupo. Because friend, even in your brokenness, there's a God-color you're meant to bring to this
world. You are part of the mosaic God is crafting together
to tell a bigger story about His love and redemption.

I pray that you'll see not only your unique wiring, but also
your life-story, as a part of the bigger picture of God's necessary work in this world.

> You are insanely valuable,
> incredibly loved, mightily gifted,
> critically needed, and awesomely
> put togetherfor a life of purpose.

Yes, you are significant, in case you missed that point, but
my guess is that you're hearing that now and it's changing
how you think about yourself and the role you play in all
your relationships and the opportunities God has put before
you.

Now it's time to go live it out.

My prayer for you is this, my friend: May today be the first
of many in which you know within the deepest parts of
your heart how special you truly are. May you, from that
point of truth, go forward with humble boldness and His
mighty power, embracing your God-color so that you shine
bright for His glory until you stand in His glorious presence
in Heaven.

Time to Lift Your Voice

Heavenly Father, thank you for the timely reminder that I will face trouble in this world. It doesn't mean there is something wrong with me. It's simply sin impacting my life and the work of the enemy seeking to undermine my life prupose. Help me, Lord, to stand strong in my faith and stay close to you. Make me steady as I seek to glorify you in the way I live. Help me grow closer to you, that you may shine bright through me in a world that needs Your light. In Jesus' Name, Amen.

Think On This

1. Maybe you've not yet had trouble in your life. If so, how do you feel about the promise of trouble?

2. If you've faced some tough stuff, how has that experience shaped you? Could there be a way that God wants to redeem your brokenness and make it a beautiful part of your God-color?

3. What steps are you willing to take in doing the hupo and growing a deep connection with God?

4. How can you take what you've learned in this study and share it with others?

Visit http://moretobe.com/mosaic-resources/ for resources to use throughout this study.

acknowledgements

Projects like this don't become a reality without two key elements — the grace of God and the support of those who share in the mission. That's why I am so thankful for my family's ongoing support and cheering from behind the scenes as well as the entire team at *More to Be* who makes bringing forth studies like this possible.

Most of all, I give glory to God who continues to overflow His love, grace, and truth throughout my heart and mind, reminding me daily to live for Him, shining my God-colors for His glory. Without Jesus, none of this would be possible.

about the author

Elisa Pulliam is a lifelong mentor, ministry leader, speaker and life coach, passionate about encouraging and equipping this generation of women to impact the next generation with relevant Truth.

After more than a decade of mothering and over 20 years of mentoring teen girls coinciding with leading women's ministries, Elisa is in tune with the struggles of teens, twenty-somethings and today's women. Having lived a life apart from God, marked by a legacy of dysfunction and a long season of rebellion, Elisa understands the power of the Cross. When she met Jesus as her Lord and Savior during her junior year of college, her life radically changed, and her life calling soon emerged.

Elisa's deepest desire is to facilitate life transformation in others by offering practical, easily accessible, and biblically sound resources to touch the heart, mind and soul.

She is the founder of More to Be, a ministry dedicated to equipping moms, engaging teens, and encouraging mentors to life a life built on biblical truth. She is also a life coach, coach instructor, and Highlands Battery consultant, eager to equip women to live transformed by God through providing her services and encouragement at elisapulliam.com. In December 2015, Elisa's first traditionally published book will be released with Waterbrook Multnomah, *Meet the New You: A 21-Day Plan for Embracing Fresh Attitudes and Focused Habits for Real Life Change.*

Elisa is refueled by speaking at women's events as well as for groups of teenagers. Her goal is to make the most of their time by capturing biblical truths through storytelling, transparently sharing her personal experiences, and tossing in a good bit of humor as she unpacks life lessons.

Elisa counts it pure joy to be Stephen's wife, who is not only her best friend but has been Christ-with-skin-on to her for nineteen years of marriage. She also considers it a privilege to train up her four children (ages 10 through 16), and admits that they have taught her the most about love, affection and total forgiveness.

Ephesians 3:7
By God's grace and mighty
power, I have been given the
privilege of serving him by
spreading this Good News.

About More to Be

More to Be is committed to seeing this generation of women and the next enter into a personal relationship with Jesus, so that they may become more bright, more beautiful, more like Him and go forth impact this world for His glory!

Through providing simple, easily accessible online resources, *More to Be* is passionate about speaking to the hearts of tween, teen, and twenty-something girls, while also influencing today's moms to be the vessels of Truth in their daughters' lives and to see Christian women step out in faith in answering the call to mentor the next generation of young women.

- Online mentoring training and study courses encourage women to follow Christ distinctly so that they may mentor biblically. Built on principles captured by Elisa Pulliam in her book, *"Impact My Life: Biblical Mentoring Simplified,"* (available on Amazon), the courses incorporate life coaching concepts with discipleship principles to equip all women to mentor.

- ETC. Mentoring and Mugs & Mornings Mentoring, presents a unique mentoring concept providing a format and collection of resources designed to equip women to lead mentoring groups in their homes and community.

- Topics & Truth FREE downloadable lessons (really curriculum without the binding) and Dig Deep Guides, provide a quick but thorough look at relevant topics steeped in biblical truth.

- Life Coaching is available especially for mentors and moms looking to develop leadership and life skills as they discover how to use their God-given gifts and talents in a variety of settings.

- The Blog is a daily landing place, full of encouragement, relevant truth, informational articles, and interesting links for today's teens, twenty-somethings, mentors, and women.

At the heart of *More to Be* is a vision to see women (young and old) become more bright, more beautiful, more like Jesus as a personally relevant God enters their lives (2 Corinthians 3:16-18 MSG) through mentoring relationships and resources grounded in biblical truth. This is what it means to experience life transformed -- a life where there is more to be as we become more like Him and impact the world around us.

If you have any questions about *More to Be*, please email more@moretobe.com or visit www.moretobe.com.

> *2 Corinthians 3:16-18 MSG*
> *. . . when God is personally*
> *present, a living Spirit. . .*
> *Nothing between us and God,*
> *our faces shining with the*
> *brightness of his face. And*
> *so we are transfigured much*
> *like the Messiah, our lives*
> *gradually becoming brighter*
> *and more beautiful as God*
> *enters our lives and we*
> *become like him.*

Have you enjoyed the journey?

I'd love to hear from you!

elisa@moretobe.com

Spread the Word

We'd love for you to share about *More to Be* and our *Engage Teen Bible Study Collection* with others!

moretobe.com

facebook.com/moretobe

twitter.com/elisapulliam

pinterest.com/elisapulliam

instagram/elisapulliam

24887651R00057

Made in the USA
Middletown, DE
09 October 2015